I0163518

ALL OF US ARE BIRDS & SOME OF US HAVE BROKEN WINGS

OJO TAIYE

Thank you for purchasing this exclusive Kingdoms' in the Wild book. To receive special offers, bonus content, and information on new releases and other great reads, sign up for our newsletter by visiting KingdomsintheWild.com

ELEGIAC: UNFINISHED DRAFT OF
HAUWA LIMAN'S HUMANITARIAN WORK

i—

what will you sing if hunger abides in your blood?
there is a name for the animal grief makes of us—
a body falls to the earth like hammered nails & all
that remains is a dirt mound melting in the rain.
for days now, i stand in Rann—a small town
painted with blood & constant fear. there is
enough fractured in this land without pretending
that home is an open prison. no words can beauty
this: i mean to say there are words you write
when you score a name with a blade. eulogy of a
body in prayer: what god turns his cheeks to see
his sweetest lambs slaughtered before they can
grow up into sheep? a boy is dying. a girl is dying.
a hundred students & a hundred healthcare
workers are dying. what can i give to be that
season, that sacred space contained in every
child's voice asking where then is safe?

O Borno, what century fell at your door? i took to my hands & knees when you climbed out from a garlic clove & kissed the moon on its cheek. it was only months when it felt like i had been grieving your *abduction* forever. i keep meaning to stop. to wait for you, night after night as my little sister does when i'm gone — i mean to say i make a list of things i know you'll come back for. i will say come back, come back for the children you left & the dog. come back, i will say to rock the newborn babies to sleep & console their depressed teenage mothers. come back for your brother & the nights full of cold bowls of oat brewed with cardamom & cloves.

last night i had a dream where i was planted at the rupture of a root where the land became your wilting petals. shouldn't we mourn for *Hauwa Liman?* i speak of a certain rooftop not far from collapse. i mark in charcoals & sense the new branches of a cypress within me waiting to tear the gauze. i look into them & see a stigma of stars falling across dark fields. there is a raven at the door: each new day i show my garnet arms & our hurts become full-blown.

OJO TAIYE— I read what happened to Hauwa Liman in the news.
PUNCHNG.COM // Alas, Nigeria fails to save her daughter
BBC.COM // Boko Haram faction kills second aid worker in Nigeria

SURVEILLANCE CAMERA

the doctor *says* my mother is suffering from retrograde amnesia & it will take long if not eight years or more for her to kiss the nape of any hunger. i press my hands against her body & listen to the war on television. a child's love is butter & milk, two thirds worry & two thirds grief. i want to believe in rebirth that what comes from loss is a form of fibrous light partitioned into many rays. my mother is a poem liable to come apart if touched without a heart. can i give her today since she has lost hold of yesterday? what is memory if not the *proper noun* for a woman caught stealing into her own body. i give my mother a new day & a spark, tell her to sift through boxes of photos & old videos & be ready to weave the welkin sphere of a body still empty with another inside. it's uncanny how much she no longer cares about her fish flick pond. she talks to herself like a witness—the stillness of moths on a vase of tulips—the shame of birds without seed.

a book lies nearby in a room filled with dust that light brings. picture this: think of a keyboard in a forgotten earth in August where someone presses the delete button. & when i thought about the petals of a dead magnolia blossom. i knew i wanted them to mean nothing & suggest everything— that we must make meaning to survive. how it feels to stand outside a house falling off this umber world. i look at my mother & see a door— where things go to lose their names. either way history does not end in borders. & i understand when people say you don't miss what you don't know, they mean there is no environmentally safe way to remember.

———

EDITION.CNN.COM // Second aid worker held by Boko Haram executed as negotiation deadline expires
NIGERIANPILOT.COM // Atiku, Saraki, others react to the murder of aide worker, Hauwa Leman
VANGUARDNGR.COM // Hauwa Liman's father hails late daughter's humanitarian work

SUNFLOWERS IN GOBI DESERT

for Ai Qing

in the year i was born, my father was a bird of exile. what is a border if you can't fly right over it? i trawl the sleep of a body, eager to haunt for love & logic in extinct places. eviction is a form of heartbreak, yes, it is—ask me for proof of parentage. the first year of exile, i smuggle my father back into a body of water forced to wander the earth in rags: from desert to desert. what's the word for a man whose child learns to shed his black hair for marigold in a country he's never lived in? i open the windows of an underground cavern built with reeducation bricks & say: who are we? why are we here? it's a common belief we evolve from grief but god knows i lost every picture of myself as a child. the fifth year of exile, my father grows lean from eating only his longings. to disinfect a memory, clean a birdhouse of plywood & store the past. my father holds a gun in his mouth & falls asleep without a halo.

a dream can clean a body like communion—*what home is for* you, country-song full of alcohol & *a poem that starts with blood where there should be birds*. in the tenth year of exile, my father is sky sick & i whispered: have you tried yelling at god's sun & everything smells like the picture of a man wearing the horizon, then bruise, then rust. this is a reminder that i was not born here. i was numbed into boyhood from a grave by some government of no mothers whose lantern still glitters in my sleep. in the eighteenth year of exile, Xinjiang province! i put the word on a page, —the privilege of a history every time i find my way around a wound that blurs into a procession of father's growing out of my body smoking the sky into meat like a dress unworn from childhood. & on the days when i can't remember, this trauma holds something like happiness & a bottle of vodka petaling into blades.

THE ONLY FOREIGN AID MY
MOTHER EVER WANTED WAS SAFETY

after the four Congo refugees who died when
their overloaded canoe capsized in Lake Albert

i kneel in the hairline light   of
exile & home. no one leaves   home
if the ocean will swallow   them   up. strange how
sitting   in a truck at the
Sebagoro   landing   site   on
Lake   Albert   shoreline
means *peace.*

yesterday   my   *mother ate her own*
appendix in a Ugandan bound pirogue. not because
hunger makes you

whole but because there is a name for grief   to grow
into. i come from a small world— a lifted paragraph
from one

                    of the worst conflict displacement
affected *shit holes.*   *i understand the need to*
define as a need for hope. In *Uturi,* my relatives are
dying;

                        not because they

            are

                    Hema or
                Bagagere, but because
they share the same land   with minerals. once this
        highland was our
birthplace.   once we were birds carrying
the sky into night.

            now i wake to red sand & follow   a trail of
            enmity & blood.

***

on the side of a road in   *Kasia* province, a
woman's
abandoned   luggage
     & a suitcase spilling out music CD's.   what
happened
to the   woman?
why is the case open? did she
manage
   to run away?

———

SURVIVORS OF DRC VIOLENCE TELL STORIES OF HORROR: ALJAZERA.COM— A recent wave of targeted attacks has left a trail of death, destruction, and mass displacement in the Democratic Republic of Congo's northeastern province of Ituri. The above poem is a sort of requiem for the symposium of endangered stars evicted to the water.

IS THIS STILL WHAT I WANT?

i gather the borders of my body with care like a burdened beast. my mouth is a gun— misfired bird grasping a fistful of air. i meant to say a poem hurts like that, doesn't it? i make home for my trauma with a giant room for joy. yes, abundant joy— another kind of reaching, so i carry myself like a true song constellated with worries: a map thumbtacked with dirty verbs because the poem about joy is mostly about wanting & wanting. last night, i couldn't sleep, so i raised my hands to make paper boats—my poems are bodies reminding me that someday i won't be home to anyone. i'm afraid to tell myself or my lover or my therapist what i need to survive— i still want to risk *pain* at the end. look how much grief is found in this queer body— at the end i want my departure to be a long poem burning, dipping in the distance calling my body a pleasure, without shame.

everything ricochets inside me. it is the season of falling & everything i do is a miracle. what is *gratitude* if not a brink of so much touching & not touching. strange how i like to watch the world crawl long & slow: my hands drag after some loss, after some inexact past that bleeds through the debris of my memory— the rhythm of a rotting plum. every morning i give grief a new language— a sister tongue. maybe it's the way i have learned to reset bird bones without breaking: a compass for dancing around this dysphoria & rose beads. i look at the image of an almost violet sunset & all i can hear is the laughter of children walking towards crashing of ocean waves. i was born to know that nothing is better than a list of beginnings & destinations— like dawn slicing the horizon into the distance of our loneliness.

POEM

for Ann

i woke up this morning & realized that what gives us life was taking it back but in small drops of falling leaves & muted days. every day i open the door & i do it by looking at my mother: one of spring's miscarriages. i was five when my mother had cancer— cervical cancer— a body soft with birdlike bones rotting like a roadkill. i imagine the cancer preening her from her bones like a vulture: the body burning into itself. little me standing in my mother's hut, heartbroken & crying in silence. the doctor *said* there is nothing we can do. the cancer—a million tiny jelly fish is spreading & spreading & spreading until she smelled of death sweat sharp as July rain on hot asphalt.

INFIBULATION

for Asiya & Khadija

i

alhamdu llillah masha' allah insha' allah & in the shadow of my grief, i say my sister's name every day. memory is the body & the unbody— sometimes i am too scared to watch my sister's bite their bones into a tenor hum that leaks gold. like light slumped over a broken window, i've lived through the ruin of my father's homeland. a language without voice in a dark buttoned up sky. dearest mother, what becomes of the girls whose doors are slammed so hard, the house fell behind them? the cattle at a ranch reminds me of most girls in Somalia. their sobs as the brand bites into their *labia*. something has snapped into two—the pianist's mis-struck chords— fragments of a dissected word. something has been lost that won't ever return— a body without—a nipped rose—a rotting—a girl was here once.

dearest mother, what becomes of the girl who desperately wants to *climax*? the language of grief so often begins with a memory. how do i explain this ruin in simple words? — she was *cut & sewn* at the age of six. what i mean: a life-long regret for *myth & misconception.* we, the daughters of Somalia are chipped walls that no one can see through a bundle of wild orchids broken at the wet seam of where all the worlds touch. *what would it take to say piss but mean pain? to say childbirth but mean fallen doors?* in the beginning, my sister was born naked & on a field that has gone un-frolicked just so i can say, there, beneath the cottonwood tree where we shared the *fava bean* in celebration of independence.

iii

i know the tongue she speaks— grief is a kind of language you can touch. i familiar the body—uncauterized wound— red & leaking. i think of my mother, her calloused hand, unfurled over my sister's tiny fist, the razor blade she teaches her to clutch. its mouth, like my grandfather's *panga*. now i imagine every child—the strange woman in a black *jellabiya—pries open, the fleshy folds steaming with blood escaping like still hot wind in summer.*

iv

let me start again, once, as a child— the scar where she was once open.

v

the strange woman smells of　　　　mercurochrome
razor blades,
　　　　cotton balls & alcohol from a plastic bag
　　　　　　　she knelt between my sister's legs
a razor in her hands
wiped my sister's pubic area　　　　with alcohol

　　　　my sister— her eyes burning
& with one swift movement
she felt the blade cutting through
　　　　her skin

vi

a frigid body,　　　a frigid existence
　　　　(there came long recurring nights when pain
would wake her up
　　　　a stack of wood keeps burning down

vii

her body into a *thin strip of sunset that still aches when her lover hooks his fingers to drag an orgasm's unsteady pulse from inside her)*

—

with adapted line from Torrin A. Greathouse

TRANSLATION BOOK FOR A CHILD
BETWEEN COUNTRIES

instead of having to say i'm falling apart because grief is easier to rename, i spend my night awake & press my back to the dark damp wood of my bed. there'd been black birds flitting above the crosshatched grass & a howl here so strong it shakes the pawpaw tree. i'm filled with the need to stay & i choose to stay this time for once with all my deep sins. the world tells me, i am a tree. i live in a spot on a train's track that leads to nowhere. i touch myself— & at the next stop, i meet a girl who wears a stain— the stain on rubble like scarves around her neck. living can be an act of loss. i don't know how to define mercy. my mother is a map of holes dressed in hooded vestment. my father is questioned for marriage fraud. my uncle dies from *self-harm* in a detention center.

my sister is a false minor— she wears white & became a shadow. my brother is a bird we return to the sky as smoke. it's funny being here & a memory of motion. i'm no one's daughter— a child with a hole in her throat. how did i get here? & in my hands, a whisper— war. what every child knows but rarely discuss. violence is my country's boyfriend. nothing else cuts the air quite like this movie of blood blinking lively like popcorns along its numb scar. what leaves you half dead? what strips the precluded fascination with flowers? what paints you in colors with the blunt edge of a practiced tongue until gray appears on your earlobes like stoned cattle? i've lost track of the times i have hope for something so simple & sweet to sip: jawbreakers. i confess i am a double ended wick & i carried it for justice & the wind.

MEMORY AS A NECESSARY PAIN

with lines from Roy Guzman

this morning, i pluck peonies from my father's throat &
watch it turn into an old lover's hand upon the water like
a moon that wouldn't heal. as a child, my country was a
roof that's always collapsing. how it spreads on my
mother's face— a brief dazzle of pink light like a rapture
in a stranger's eyes. how memory is a heart that has
forgotten to sing— a bare precis & the isolation that any
alignment of pain can trigger when they are carved out
of grief. what do you do when your body is a pistol or rifle
pulled apart? since most of us bloomed out of sorrow like
swans always bent on pond water. i am afraid of
attending a place now green with mold but still edible for
some. after dinner with a friend who dreams of dragons
dancing over a fence. i come home to touch my sister's
sweltering body & i am imagining how one can ride a
bullet toward eternity with a Greek   of soul. even now, i
open up & shut like a house with only hurricanes moving
through it. reminding me of communion as a child where
we'll stop to mislay our moistures on other's necks.

THE SOUND YOU MAKE WHEN YOU LOOK AT ME

i push play on another scene
from that movie where your skin
dissolves like a tablet of powder
in the rain, there is something about
distance & the heart growing fonder
always being the one left behind
& never the one leaving   i want to
spend a day not thinking about flowers
still waiting to be born around bones
that used to hold other bodies
inside them... my body is a carnival
on fire, a mouth stuffed with lilacs

it is hard to breathe in a world full of cars
that get into accidents   run your hand
through my hair & tell the birds
to go south forever
do you ever get lonely   have you ever
been afraid to hold on   does the smoke
stay in your clothes like as it stays in mine
name this sometimes-unwanted-part of
me— how a grave & i share the same
unclean throat like water with a smell
of the north in my memory tying knots
as part of a ritual for a lover who had
lost everything but the taste
of bitterness & dry bread

ALL OF US ARE BIRDS
& SOME OF US HAVE BROKEN WINGS

the morning gives us leftovers from a night filled with a thousand *Dapchi* children melting into fertile soil. this nation calls my body a crime— a light house on the lips of bomb shelters. today a boy told me that girls are just places to crawl through to get to somewhere else. & i pretend it means i was born to live under water. i name each of my knuckles after a country that contains my happiness— a shoreline where i can dip my head into the water & emerge unbroken. i know no other name to give to the waves or maybe we don't name grief with things that can die: paper dolls sing in my dreams. my uncle finds a home by throwing a match in every corner of his body. to embrace the dark is to glow.

i—

what kind of world should we leave for our children? history is a place in my skin. the sky bloodies with birds & i swallow my left hand until a country leaves me like a stolen car. deduct a *soft war* from my mouth & it's a buttonhole cracked open like a window: an evidence of my body keeping alive its erasures.

ii—

blood, more blood & i will never know how carnage lunges inside a woman except the woman is my mother scattering her sons like salt. what the war costs, a son must pay out of his body & a river lassoes my father's body into a forest biblical with bones. no one told me what the war was for & i pledge my house to the fire. how if you look closely enough, every war-child was once a prayer waking an ache in my jaw.

iii—

my old country gives me a hammer when i ask for
a home & i imagine the bloodbath as a sunset in a
razed village. in this poem, my birth rhymes with
pogrom & language is the house i swallow the
keys to. when i consider that disaster begins
inside a mouth: i taste salts afterwards & trace
where my sister is a body buried in brown &
fragile skin.

iv—

my grandfather says girlhood was the child he
was never allowed to raise & sews a *fork* into my
hand. i wear my blood as bracelets & my brothers
suckle on the udders of guns. listen: i boil a broth
of stars until the sun wounds the sky—my uncle
has no son to carry his blood home. distance is
another way to measure my mother's body
homing in my head like panga cuts. i remind
myself to water the battle ground until every sea
bulging to the shore with our blood is the edge of
a knife i teach the depth of my pain.

MOTHS & ORIGAMI CHILDREN

i taste my mother's sickness
in my mouth & analyze
the spittle:
                (grief lies folded
      in a woman's hand)
what we've left behind
can be disturbing

          can i touch your throat?
a pile of daylight composed
of many meanings
names emerge from the center
of each thing—   love. butterfly
      fields of daisies. mother
      blood. moths are burning mid-flight
      & you whisper *folding into origami children*

we name parts of our body after
flowers—we carry the dead like seeds
      we carry our wounds like
            orifices

i want to write a poem

that will have a woman's
            pulse inside
first verse: you get smaller as you lose your heart
second verse: shovel off the dirt of buried
            memories— *you should be tired of chewing*
            the same bones day in & *day out*
third verse: try holding your breath for infinity
fourth verse: each drop of love is like a sunset
            in the mouth of a stranger
last verse: spend less of life attached to the absence
                  hook up a poem directly to your heart

A HUNDRED SILENT BURST

for Chukwuemeka Kachi

you ken the language of *pain*
as a seed within a keel—
within cupped hands

seizure— a word waved at you
from a dictionary & then
it removes its arm

& sinks back into your eyes,
to wood & pulp depths
through guts & spine

of bone-dry pages.
you licked the fingers of coated pills
hunted back & forward

to mislay & to suffer impairment.
to be absent & forlorn
to calcify like light & bubbles

from a plastic wand.
to spiral into the air into a thousand
silent bursts with black arms

& twig teeth
                    engulfing you

———

I made this homage collage by sewing favorite adapted lines belonging
to Layli Long Soldier to lines of my own

IT IS THE SEASON OF FALLING & ALL I CAN REMEMBER IS THE TASTE OF MY MOTHER'S LAUGHTER

with adapted lines from Bryce Emely

my life is a list of perfect water songs. today, a man told me to breathe. to become something so light like joy— the only thing holier than a moth's wing. the truth is i'm sick of drawing a country of memories with thick red lines—how i must be in some way, a list of all my father lost while living. somewhere in the middle of my life, i'm listening to songs not made for me— i always mean a river *because we have to hold our fathers like storms inside us.* is it wrong to speak of what happens at night? *i learned from my mother to object to nothing except a man who holds his wife by the throat like a bouquet of waterlilies.* once in a dream, i dropped all my skin down a well to make the water rise. what we call grief i call a dry basin.

what we call memory i call a form of intimacy: a longing to feel with no weight ripple the surface. there is a house by the sea wearing my father's skin like an ethos & outside my window the blooming magnolia carries me toward another childhood where i trade my losses for a landscape made of teeth. i storyboard origin: the sky is September blue & a woman on a sinking ship is a life raft— i don't think i've ever written the word *hope,* but nothing else fits here. i've seen whole orchids blooming from ash— which is to say, i have stopped looking for myself in movies. how do you end a poem reminding you so much about your mother? where do you keep the souls of the dead building a nest in your bones? look, the leaves are falling again. & all the years of waiting to say goodbye are nameless now.

OJO TAIYE IN CONVERSATION

MANY OF THE POEMS IN THIS CHAPBOOK DEAL WITH HISTORY, MEMORIES AND BORDERS. WHAT ABOUT THOSE SUBJECTS INTERESTS YOU?

I have always been obsessed with the idea of past lives, embodying memories, borders and the idea of past traumas. I always feel I interact with these thematic tropes in a different way than reading it or understanding it in a literal way; the fragmentation and the precariousness of memory (both personal and national) and how trauma becomes diffused and spans many, many bodies. There is so much violence that lives within people's bodies and memories. I consciously wanted to write about them from the perspective of extreme distance (literally, physically) and extreme closeness (incarnation, contagion, and inside the mind as it fragments). Also, I find writing about memory as an object, as something that has shape, something I need to give an outline so as not to forget. This sublime longing for what is past is both a weight and a kind of time travel for me—a sort of an overpouring, a mirroring of trauma's reverberations.

YOU SPEAK ABOUT YOUR POETRY IN CONNECTION TO ELEGY, WHICH HAS A LONG AND DEEP HISTORY: HOW DID YOU END UP AT THAT PARTICULAR FORM?

I've always thought all poetry is elegiac in some way. I took to poetry following the 2016 death of my sweet mother, which was a paralyzing loss. When life is taken, rage sets in. It's undeniably true that all my poems have become elegies, even my love poems. I write because I don't want to forget, especially not my mother. Yet, I would say that being able to imagine elegy (as an origin of inquiry) is important to me. Even then, I hold this thought close: that it's possible to grieve something you've never seen. I definitely don't want to glamorize and romanticize violence or desensitize readers to it. I am only interested in the huge gap between grief as it is experienced and grief as it is remembered.

YOUR WORK HOLDS BOTH BEAUTY AND DARKNESS, MUCH LIKE LIFE. WHERE DO YOU DRAW YOUR INSPIRATIONS AND INFLUENCES FROM?

Often, it's just a philosophical ideal, playful, lyrical, surprising language, or a small moment that serves as an entry way. A good first line; the usual sort of thing. I've always been drawn to stories about abandonment, departure, borderlines, intergenerational trauma, separation, sexual violence, immigrant /migration stories and loss. Again, there are a few poets I often turn to for motivation which is one of the reasons that I write and continue to exist. These artists include: Aria Aber, Ocean Vuong, Ilya Kaminsky, Lucille Clifton, Sam Sax, Hieu Ming Nguyen, Kristin Chang. Devin Kelly, C.T Salazar.

HOW IMPORTANT IS LANGUAGE AND/OR WORD CHOICE TO YOUR WRITING?

What drew me to poetry was probably the permission/agency it gave me to disrupt language and reinvent it for myself. I think especially, for those of us whose histories have been erased by colonization, the white washing of history, the expectation and standards of the West, and capitalism, to name a few. Language helps me to fantastically re-imagine what's possible; rebuild a world that don't just replicate my realities but reinvent them and re-story them. And also, to identify myself (my ancestry and heritage included), in a world of so much multiplicity and marginalization, where labels and movements seem to matter above individuality and self-discovery. Of course, language has its own texture. Word choices for me refer to the material things in the world, the things we perceive so vividly with our senses and what my poetry attempts not only to depict but to grapple with.

YOUR POEM *THE ONLY FOREIGN AID MY MOTHER EVER WANTED WAS SAFETY* PLAYS WITH SPACE AND FORM. DID YOU DECIDE BEFORE HAND THE SHAPE OR STRUCTURE OF THE POEM, OR DID THAT COME LATER?

The lineation came naturally as I was writing the poem. I find sparser lines quieter and more reserved if I want a poem to convey anything like stillness or poems that make me feel fragmented in a way. I think I just mean that white space can be tactile.

HOW DOES SUBJECT MATTER INFLUENCE THE FORMAT OF YOUR POEMS?

Not like it does for me, but I like to think that form and subject matter interact and shape each other in really dynamic ways that are hard to define, if that makes sense.

IT GOES WITHOUT SAYING THAT POEMS ARE NOT ALWAYS STRICTLY AUTOBIOGRAPHIC, HOW MUCH OF YOUR WORK DEALS WITH THE BIOGRAPHY OF SELF?

As someone who engages so intensely with trauma and identity, I have actually been thinking that most of my work hinges on navel-gazing. I never sat down thinking to myself that I would write about loss, suicide or even trauma— as it relates with the biography of self. These things just emerge. They are hidden   fixations and I didn't have another way to excise them. And I think every poem is trying to summon a self and a lot of times the poems are more memorials to that process than products created through juxtaposing bits of language from divergent and competing registers. I realized my poems comprise a kind of anti-philosophy that value material presence; a kind of self-communion that unties that which is supposedly social or political from the autobiographical. All of this is formed by a word like "solidarity," but also informed by a word like "community". All that comes together to form the resonant source behind so much of what I write about— the everyday life.

WHAT IS AN OBSCURE THING YOU FIND INTERESTING ABOUT THE WORLD?

The light at dusk. Even though I think of a literally grounded sense of nostalgia, belonging & homecoming.

WHAT ODD, FUNNY OR INTERESTING FACT CAN YOU SHARE ABOUT YOUR WRITING HABITS OR PROCESS?

Because I never had any formal training, I was never taught how to have a writing practice. Until recently I only write on a laptop because I like to play with language and see what grows from what at first looks like nothing. When I write, I sometimes start with the philosophical ideal, but just as often I let it develop organically as I write, then hone it in revision. I often write at night.

IS THERE SOMETHING YOU FIND PARTICULARLY DIFFICULT ABOUT THE WRITING PROCESS?

Y'know, I can say all the cliché things about writing being a cathartic process or I can just say, writing is hard work. Along with its unending rejections, I feel like writing is another path to being lonely.

WHAT OTHER ART FORM [IF ANY] INFLUENCES OR INFORMS YOUR WRITING? *E.G. FILM, MUSIC, PAINTING / VISUAL ART...*

Film, especially documentary. I am always striving to find the sweeping historical underpinnings in the little, intimate story depicted in these documentaries.

WHAT'S AN UNDERRATED (OR LITTLE RECOGNIZED) BOOK YOU LOVE?

Well, almost all the poetry books I have laid my hands on are widely recognized, except for "The New Man"— it was authored by a Nigerian Journalist. I felt so passionately about the book that I became obsessed with its subject matter. The poems included, are energetic, and they claw.

WHAT ARE YOU WORKING ON NOW AND WHERE CAN READERS FIND MORE WORKS BY YOU?

To be honest, my current project is very green, but here is my best take: I am working on poems about climate change and thinking about its practical underpinnings as well as its overarching effect on man & his environment. It's a sort of poetry/hybrid project called *Mother Drought Migration*. It's still very much a work in progress.

ARTIST STATEMENT: Ojo Taiye is the author of *All of Us are Birds and Some of Us have Broken Wings"* selected as winner of the KITW Annual Poetry Prize. His poetry has been published or forthcoming in *Rattle, Cincinnati Review, Grain, Banshee, SavantGarde, Litmag, Glintmoon, Willow Springs, Lambda Literary, Cherry Tree, Ruminate, Gargouille Magazine, Ninth letter, Vallum, Frontier Poetry, Palette, Stinging fly, Notre Dame Review, Tinderbox Poetry, Strange Horizon and elsewhere.* His poem *"There Is Nothing You Can Do to Replace My Fada"* is the winner of the 2019 Jack Grape Poetry Prize; His poem "Elegiac" is the winner of the 2019 Hart Crane Poetry Prize. His work has been nominated for *Best of the Net.* He is currently living in Nigeria. You can follow him on twitter @ojo_poems

MORE FROM KINGDOMS IN THE WILDS

Red Chapel by Catherine Hou
Sorrow by Saiteru S.
Roots Grew Wild by Erica Hoffmeister

KINGDOMS IN THE WILD PRESS LLC: Is the place for original, experimental, and cutting-edge poetry and fiction. We strive to bring you work that reflects the world's complex and intertwined cultures and histories. Read works by wonderful writers and poets by visiting our website: KINGDOMSINTHEWILD. COM